DropBox User Guide for Seniors

How to use Dropbox for Beginners

Mary C. Hamilton

Copyright© 2021

All rights reserved

No part of this book shall be reproduced, edited, and transmitted without the prior notice of the author and publishers.

Dedicated

To

John

Mark

Luke

Natasha

I love you all...

Acknowledgment

I want to thank my colleagues at *TechVerse* for their support and contributions in making this work a success...

Contents

Introduction 9
chapter 1 11
Get Dropbox 11
How to Install Dropbox 12
To install Dropbox on a computer: 12
To install Dropbox on a smartphone: 13
How to register and sign in into Dropbox 14

Chapter 2 16
The simple basics of using Dropbox 16
How to save file for offline viewing 17

Chapter 3 20
Creating and Using folder on Dropbox 20
Create a folder 21
Upload files to folder 23
Move folders / files into folder 25
How to Delete Files or folder 27
How to Download files on Dropbox 30
How to Add a shared folder to your Dropbox account 32
How to add a shared file to Dropbox 35
How to share links on Dropbox 37

Share link from Dropbox.com 37
Share link from Dropbox folder on PC 38
How to share link with Smartphone 39
Share link using the Desktop app 40
Manage shared storage space 42
Managing your Dropbox Sharing Permissions 44
How to assign member access on a shared folder: .45

Chapter 4 48
The Third Party Integrations 48
Import Videos and Photos from Facebook 49
How to connect/Disconnect Third party apps on your Dropbox 52

Chapter 5 54
Dropbox Tips and Tricks 54
Request files from people directly to Dropbox 55
Get Deleted shared folder back 57
Work as a team on files 58
Monitor Recent activities on files 60
Increase sync speed 61
Smart and Fast Bookmarks on Dropbox 63
Create and Share Screenshots instantly on Dropbox 65
How to use Background Uploading 67

How to use Drobpox Camera upload feature 69

ON Mobile: Turn Camera Uploads ON 70

The Unoffical Dropbox FAQ's 72

About the Author 85

Introduction

At one point or the other, many of us would likely have heard the word Dropbox. In fact, when we get a new computer or smartphone, or probably trying to access a file online, we would see the Dropbox logo pop up.

Dropbox is one of the world's most renowned cloud Wizards. With Dropbox, you have one of the smartest online workspace you could ever dream about.

With Dropbox, your files are easier to sync, you know, access from one device to another, anywhere and anytime. With time and innovation, Dropbox has gone beyond the handling of files online. Now, if you run a business, you can use Dropbox for easier product designs and save time to focus on work that matters.

As we take you through the simple basics of using Dropbox for personal or Professional levels, we hope that you would become better equipped to increase your work productivity.

CHAPTER 1

GET DROPBOX

How to Install Dropbox

For many new devices, Dropbox came pre-installed. So you won't probably need to install Dropbox. Although you may need to update the app is a newer version is already in the appstore.

However, for devices without Dropbox, you would have to have it installed before you can begin to enjoy the Dropbox goodies.

To install Dropbox on a computer:

1. Head over to your app store if you use a Windows or Apple device

2. Search for **Dropbox**

3. Download and complete the installation process.

To install Dropbox on a smartphone:

1. For Apple or Android devices, click the playstore app or apple store apple

2. Search for Dropbox

3. Download the app and wait for the installation process to get completed.

Now, you are set to begin exploring the world of possibilities with Dropbox.

How to Register and Sign in into Dropbox

To create an account on Dropbox:

1. Click on the **Sign up** button

2. You can also go to http://dropbox.com and hit the **create account** option

3. Input your name and email address in the field provided. Take note that your email address would serve as your username for Dropbox

4. In the **password field,** type a unique password you can easily remember

5. As usual, select the "term and condition" box

6. And finally click the **Create an Account** option.

CHAPTER 2

THE SIMPLE BASICS OF USING DROPBOX

How to Save File for Offline Viewing

Saving files for offline viewing helps to eliminate the stress of signing into Dropbox to access your files. Now, without internet connection, you can still open files on Dropbox stored on your device.

For Android Devices

First, you will have to *turn on* the option for **Available Offline**. When you do this;

- Your files are saved directly to your device

- Your files are also regularly updated and sync even when you make changes to any of them

- Quicker access to your files when you need them.

To do this:

1. Locate the file you would like to save for offline viewing

2. From the list, hit the arrow facing downwards just at the right side of the file's name

3. You will see the **Available offline** option. Just hit it to make the file available for offline viewing

For IOS devices

Apple users are not left out. If you use an iPad or iPhone, you can enjoy the offline availability option by:

1. Search for the file you would like to view even without turning your internet connection on

2. Then hit the three dot … just close to the file's name

3. Out of all the options that appear, you will see **Make Available offline**

4. Select the option and you're good to go.

Chapter 3

Creating and Using folder on Dropbox

CREATE A FOLDER

Folders are useful when grouping different files together. You can create a folder for files that serve the same purpose or are needed for something else.

To do this,

1. Using your browser, sign into your Dropbox account

2. You will see a grid icon on the top-right corner of your browser's screen, hit the icon

3. The select **New folder**

4. To specify what type of files you want to add to the folder, why not include a folder name?!

5. Then click **Create.**

UPLOAD FILES TO FOLDER

After creating a folder, the next thing to do is to upload and group selected files to the folder.

To do this:

1. Sign in into Dropbox, if you've not done so already

2. In the left sidebar of your browser's screen, select **All files**

3. Now hit the folder name you've just created or any other available folder you would like to keep the selected files

4. Select **Upload files**

5. Choose the particular file you would like to upload

6. Then hit **open.**

MOVE FOLDERS / FILES INTO FOLDER

If you would like to further group different folders into one:

1. From your Dropbox account, click on **All files**

2. On the folder you would like to send into a new folder, select the three dots (…) next to it

3. Well, if you intend to move multiple files or folders at once into a new folder, hover your cursor on all the folders you want to move and then check the boxes that appears. Then hit the three dotted icon to the right

4. Then select **move**

5. Choose the folder you would like to move things in

6. Finally, Select **Move.**

How to Delete Files or Folder

If you do not need a certain file anymore, why not just delete it? This would save you a lot of space on your Dropbox account. However, deleted files can still be restored within a certain time frame.

To delete files

On your Browser

1. Input your sign in details at Dropbox.com

2. In the left sidebar on your screen, select All files

3. Locate the file or folder you wish to delete, hover over it and click the three dots (...)

4. Tap **Delete**

5. Select **Delete** again.

On The Mobile App

1. Launch your Dropbox mobile app

2. Locate the file or folder you would like to delete

3. Hit the three dots(...) next to it

4. Then tap the **delete** option.

To delete files permanently

It should be noted that when you follow this routine, you won't see the folder or file anymore. Also, you can also get to delete folders or files that you own. Shared files cannot be deleted.

To do this:

1. You'll have to follow the same process of deleting files or folders as already mentioned

2. After deleting the file, click on **deleted files** just at the left sidebar of your browser

3. You'll find a box next to the file or folder, check the box

4. Select **Permanently Delete**

5. Click again to confirm.

How to Download Files on Dropbox

Sometimes, the preview function on Dropbox might not work on certain files. If you have an app on your device that support such files on Dropbox, you can download the files straight to your computer or mobile directly.

To do this:

1. Sign in to your Dropbox account

2. Select **All files** just at the left sidebar on your screen

3. Choose the file you want to download and click it

4. Select the three dots (...) at the button right of your screen

5. Then hit the Download option.

After the download is successful open the file using your **Finder** on mac or File Explorer on Windows.

How to Add a Shared Folder to Your Dropbox Account

After being invited to a shared folder, you can only access it by adding it to your account.

To do so via the sharing Tab

1. Using your browser, go to Dropbox.com

2. Select **Shared** just at the left sidebar of your browser

3. Select the shared folder you want to open

4. Hit the three dots [...] just close to the folder

5. Select **Add**

You can also add via notification from Dropbox:

1. Go to dropbox.com and sign into your account

2. Select the notification bell

3. Then hit the **add to Dropbox** option under the shared folder you want to open.

If you get a shared folder invitation and you don't operate a Dropbox account, you won't be allowed access. Kindly open a new account and verify your email address.

Any shared folder added to your account are in sync with other folder members.

How to add a shared file to Dropbox

Apart from shared folder, you can also receive invitations for shared files either through emails or via your notification on Dropbox.

The good thing about shared files is that they do not affect your storage space except if you download them to your Dropbox account.

To view all your shared files:

1. Go to Dropbox.com and sign in

2. At the left sidebar, hit the **Shared** option

3. Select **files** tab.

4. You would see all your shared files by invitation. Select any file to preview it.

How to Share Links on Dropbox

Creating and sharing links is a good way of giving people access to your file while still protecting your privacy.

Another benefit of link sharing is that many people can view your files at once and they won't be able to edit the original files.

There are various methods you can use to share links on your Dropbox account.

Share link from Dropbox.com

1. On your browser, go to http://Dropbox.com and sign in

2. On the left sidebar, select **All files**

3. Move your cursor over the file you wish to share and select the share icon

4. Select **Create link** (if a link hasn't been generated for the file already) or hit the **copy link** (if a link has been generated for the file)

5. After the above step, you will have the link copied to your clip box. Send it as messages or emails to anyone you want to access it.

Share link from Dropbox folder on PC

1. On your computer, open the Dropbox folder

2. Do a right-click on the folder or file you'd like to share

3. Hit the **Share** option

4. Select **Create a link** or **Copy link**

5. Now from your Clipboard, send link to anyone you wish.

How to share link with Smartphone

1. On the Dropbox app on your device, go to the file or folder you would like to share

2. Click on the three dots (...)

3. Hit the **Share option**

4. Select **Create a link**

5. Send link via Email, Whatsapp, Telegram or any other available methods for you.

Share link using the Desktop app

1. Launch the Dropbox app on your computer

2. On the menu bar, click the Dropbox icon

3. Hover over any folder or file you would like to share

4. Next to the older, select the three dots

5. Select share

6. Choose to either Create a link or Copy link

7. Send the copied from your clipboard.

MANAGE SHARED STORAGE SPACE

Dropbox gives users the ability to manage their own shared space. You can thus limit access for other users on when and how to use your files or folders.

1. Open Dropbox folder on your personal computer

2. Do a right-click on the shared folder

3. Hit the **select** option

4. Select the **Settings** icon

5. You will see different preferences to tweak using the drop down just close to the **Manage** access option

6. Select and unselect settings that meets your taste

7. Then hit the **Save** option.

MANAGING YOUR DROPBOX SHARING PERMISSIONS

This feature is often useful if your share a specific folder with someone. You can decide the limit of their actions on the folder.

Three roles exist for members of a shared folder:

Owner: If you create a shared folder, you thus become the owner of the folder

Viewer: a member who is a viewer cannot edit, delete or add a file to a shared folder. Such one can only view and comment on a file

Editor: an editor can add, delete or edit a file on the shared folder.

How to assign member access on a shared folder:

On the Dropbox website:

1. Sign into your account

2. In the left sidebar, hit **All files**

3. Hover your cursor over the name of the shared folder and hit the **Share icon**

4. **Select {X} people have access**

5. Select the name of the member you want to manage access

6. Click the dropdown next to the name of the member and choose **Can edit** or **Can View** option.

On a smartphone

1. If you use the Dropbox app on your phone, launch it

2. Locate the folder you want to share

- If you use an Android, hit the download arrow

- For IOS devices, hit the three dots [...] just under the folder's name

3. Hit the **share** option

4. Click the Dropdown next to the name of the member and change his/her permission settings

5. Then tap **save.**

Chapter 4

The Third Party Integrations

IMPORT VIDEOS AND PHOTOS FROM FACEBOOK

Keep your gallery every closer to you than ever before with the Facebook file integration feature. What this means in simple grammar is that you can now view all your pictures and upload on Dropbox without going through the stress of searching for them on your Facebook timeline.

If you also intend to share these files to friends and loved ones, then this is one great feature you should take advantage of.

To import Facebook files:

1. Go to Facebook.com with your browser and sign into your account

2. Hit the three line icon at the top right part of your screen, on mobile or the downward arrow icon on Desktop. The icon displays your Facebook account menu

3. Click on **Settings & Privacy**

4. Select **Settings**

5. Hit **Your Facebook Information**

6. You would see **Transfer a Copy of your Photos or Videos.** Click the option. If prompted, input your password

7. Hit the Arrow close to **Choose Destination** and pick **Dropbox** from options that displays

8. Choose whether you want to import videos or pictures and select **Next**

9. Now open Dropbox and sign in to your account to allow Facebook Data Transfer complete the process

10. Finally, select **Confirm transfer** All your photos and videos, if you select them too, would be transferred from your Facebook account to your Dropbox account.

How to Connect/Disconnect Third Party Apps on Your Dropbox

To do this,

1. Log into your Dropbox account

2. In the upper right part of your screen, select the avatar containing your profile picture or initials

3. **Select Settings**

4. You would find the **Connected Apps** tab

5. Then select the **connect** button next to any app you would to add to your Dropbox.

Disconnect a third party app from your Dropbox account

To do this:

1. Log into your Dropbox account

2. Select the Avatar containing either your initials or profile picture

3. Select **Settings**

4. Click on **Connected apps**

5. Select the arrow close to the app you would like to disconnect from your Dropbox account

6. And finally, hit the **Disconnect** button.

CHAPTER 5

DROPBOX TIPS AND TRICKS

REQUEST FILES FROM PEOPLE DIRECTLY TO DROPBOX

If you need a file from someone who doesn't use Dropbox, rather than leaving Dropbox or using an alternative method, you can get the file directly to you Dropbox account.

With Dropbox **file requests** feature, you can receive any file no matter the size right into your Dropbox account>

To request for any files:

1. Sign into your Dropbox account

2. From the left sidebar, hit the **File request**

3. **Click create a file request**

4. Briefly describe the request and select **Change folder.** This would specify where the received file would be stored

5. Select **Next**

6. A link would be generated for you. Copy the link and share to anyone you want to request a file.

You can always share by email or any other means that are convenient for you.

GET DELETED SHARED FOLDER BACK

If you mistakenly leave or delete a shared folder from your Dropbox account, you can get it back with ease.

To do so:

1. Log into your Dropbox account

2. Hit **Sharing** at the left sidebar of your browser

3. Locate the **Folders you can add to Dropbox** Section.

4. Then select any folder you would like to re-join

5. Select **Add.**

WORK AS A TEAM ON FILES

With Dropbox you can organize a team to work on files at any time and convenience. This feature is useful especially if you run an organization or host tutorial sessions for students.

Everybody on the group would get to see any shared file from you via one unique shared folder.

To create one team Dropbox folder:

1. Log into your Dropbox account

2. From the left sidebar, hit **Team**

3. Then hit create free room

4. Type in a unique name for the team, and hit the **Create a new team Dropbox** feature

5. Then fill in the email address and password for the team

6. Hit **Continue**

7. You can always invite other members to join your team via the invite links.

8. Hit **Continue** and select **Create team Dropbox** to finish.

Monitor Recent Activities on Files

Rather than searching on looking for files you've just worked on recently, you can easily pull them up with ease if you need to modify or view them.

1. Open the drop box app or log into your account

2. On the left side bar, you will see **Recents**

3. Select it.

In this section, you will see the last files you've accessed. You can also choose to download, share, and comment or even delete other versions of your files from this section.

INCREASE SYNC SPEED

Dropbox app is actually optimized to avoid interfering with your network speed. What this means is that it uses less internet bandwidth for your other internet needs to operate seamlessly, thus syncing at a lower speed.

You can get Dropbox to operate faster on your device if you intend to only focus on Dropbox for that period of time.

To change Dropbox Bandwidth settings:

1. Open your system tray

2. Do a right click on the **Dropbox** icon

3. Hit the **gear** icon and select **Preferences**

4. Hit the **Bandwidth** tab

5. Under **upload rate** choose **Don't Limit.**

This would speed up the sync or upload process for Dropbox.

Smart and Fast Bookmarks on Dropbox

Keeping your bookmarks on your browser can muddle your browser and make it clumsy, especially if you're the bookmark type.

The best way to avoid this, is by keeping your bookmarks on the cloud. In that way, you can save as many bookmarks as possible and refer to them later, when in need.

To easily do this:

1. Open Dropbox and create a folder for Bookmarks. You can decide to give it any name you want

2. When you are surfing the web with your browser, at the website bar (top of the screen where the website link is shown), also known as the location bar, drag it into your Dropbox tab

3. Then finally drop the link into the created folder for Bookmarks.

Create and Share Screenshots Instantly on Dropbox

Sharing Screenshots have never been easier with the Dropbox share feature. Now you can avoid dragging screenshots into folder before sharing the links to people.

The key is to enable Dropbox screenshot sharing option.

To do this:

1. Open your system tray

2. Do a right click on the Dropbox icon

3. Hit the gear icon and select **Preferences**

4. Select the **import** tab

5. Check the **share screenshot using Dropbox box**

6. And select **ok**

7. When you take screenshots, Dropbox automatically saves them to the **Dropbox/screenshot** path.

8. The link for the screenshot is also automatically copied into your clipboard

9. Share this link to anybody you want.

How to use Background Uploading

Enable **Background Uploading** if you want photos to automatically upload to Dropbox anytime you change location.

However, you can also stop it if you want especially to save battery of your dive when in low battery mode.

1. Launch your Dropbox app

2. Go to the **Camera Upload** section

3. Hit **Background uploading**

4. Select the battery level you want **Background uploading to stop.** You can set **Only while phone is charging** toggle to on

5. Then hit **ok.**

How to use Dropbox Camera Upload Feature

If you want to save exciting scenes for longer period of time, then make use of the Dropbox camera upload feature. With this feature, your photos are uploaded directly to your Dropbox account. You can thus move them to any folder you wish.

To change your Camera Upload preferences:

1. Locate **System Preferences** on your Dropbox account

2. Hit on **Security and Privacy**

3. Select the **Privacy** tab

4. Select **Files and Folders**

5. Under **Removable volumes,** Check or uncheck preferences.

ON Mobile: Turn Camera Uploads ON

If you use an Apple Device:

1. Launch the Dropbox app on your smartphone

2. At the right bottom part of your screen, select **Account**

3. Select **Camera Uploads**

4. Toggle the camera upload option ON

5. Hit upload to start uploading photos.

For Android Devices:

1. Launch your Dropbox app

2. Hit the **Menu** button

3. Select **settings**

4. Hit the **Turn on Camera Uploads** just under the Camera upload option

5. Then hit **allow.**

THE UNOFFICAL DROPBOX FAQ'S

Q: Is Dropbox Secure and Private?

A: Yes, Dropbox is secure for your files and workspace. Dropbox has a security team that is dedicated, using top level security protocols to backup and protect your private files.

With the latest two-step verification, you can also add another level of security to your signing in process on Dropbox.

One unique feature of Dropbox is that other Dropbox users cannot see your saved files without your permission. The only way they can access your stuffs is if you give them a personal link to your files or folders.

Q: Are my Photos and Videos still on Facebook platform after I transferred them to Dropbox?

A: Only copies of your files are actually sent to your Dropbox account. You can still find all your Photos and Videos on your Facebook account

Q: Can Facebook Data Transfer be used to Transfer Files into a Dropbox Business account?

A: If your Dropbox plan is a Business Plan, then you want to keep it strictly for work. Therefore, the Data Transfer tool from Facebook won't work with it.

Q: Can the third-party apps access all my information?

Linked third party apps to your Dropbox account will have access to your basic information, for example, your email address. Other times, the type of information accessed by third party apps depends on the purpose of the app. Some apps can request for permission in editing, viewing or managing your folders and files.

To individually track each third party app and see their requested information on your account:

1. On your web browser, log in to your Dropbox account

2. Click on your avatar or display picture in the upper right part of your screen

3. Select **Settings**

4. Select **Connected apps**

5. Choose the app you would like to track. Next to **permissions**, you'll see the app access.

Q: Why can't I Preview my file?

A: The good thing about previewing files is that it helps to conserve storage. Rather than just downloading any file that is being shared to you, why not simply preview it first before you decide whether to download or not?

However, some people get the error message when trying to preview a file on Dropbox.

If you cannot preview a file, it could be that the file type is not supported by Dropbox, check that your file type is supported.

Troubleshooting Shared links

Some people complained that their shared link isn't working and it is showing a 404 error message. If you ever got the error message, here are things you can do to resolve the issue:

1. Delete files: If you delete the file after sharing the link, people cannot access it any longer. However, if you restore the deleted file, the link would begin working.

2. Disabled link: Any disabled link ceases to function. To check if any link is disabled:

- Open Dropbox

- In the left sidebar, select **Shared**

- Hit the **Links** tab

- Next to the link you're having problems with, select the three dots (…)

- Select **Links settings**

- Select **Link for editing** or **Link for Viewing**

- Check if **Disable downloads** toggle is on

- Toggle off

3. Expired links: Using a Dropbox professional or Business account, you can set an expiry period for your links. If you set an expiry period,

create a new link for your folder of file if the time is passed.

4. Rewinded your Dropbox account: If you shared a link and then rewind your Dropbox account, it may cause the link to stop working. You can:

- Go to your Shared links page

- Hit the three dots {...} close to the link giving you issues

- Hit **Delete link**

- Then proceed to create a new shared link to the folder of file.

Camera Upload isn't working?

Try out these simple troubleshooting tips if you get an error message while using camera uploads:

⇒ Inspect your internet connection

- A slower internet connection can slow down camera uploads

- You can try connecting to a faster Wi-Fi network

⇒ Get your battery fully charged

- Uploads are usually slower on low battery

- Try connecting your device to a power source and charge your battery

⇒ Update to the latest version of Dropbox

⇒ Stop other apps simultaneously using your device's camera.

ABOUT THE AUTHOR

MARY HAMILTON is the CEO of *TechVerse*, a renowned software developing organization formed by tech gurus from around the world.

She is also a tech and gadget reviewer, who has written numerous "how-to" manuals for users to get to know their devices better.

Top magazines and tech websites have referenced most of her books as the gold standard for "User guides."

Enjoying her life in a small town in Texas, where she lives with her only daughter, Mary continues to write best-seller books to help improve the tech world.

Made in the USA
Las Vegas, NV
22 June 2023